SPECIAL REPORT

Why submitting a Physician's Report (VRS-6B) and copies of your medical records may not be enough to prove your Virginia Retirement System (VRS) disability retirement benefits claim

What you (and your doctor) don't know can hurt you!

Printed in the United States of America

ISBN: 978-0-9976374-0-3

Important Disclaimer

This Special Report is not legal advice specific to your particular situation! It is intended to educate you and to help you identify certain pitfalls and traps, but please do NOT take anything in this book to be legal advice. Because of the rapidly changing nature of the law, information contained in this Special Report may become outdated. As a result, it is best to consult with an experienced disability attorney when you are thinking about applying for Virginia Retirement System (VRS) disability retirement benefits.

Are You Represented?

We do not want to interfere with any legal relationship you may have now. If you are already represented by a lawyer, this Special Report may raise certain questions for you. Please discuss your questions with your lawyer.

Table of contents

Introduction

If you are a member of the Virginia Retirement System (VRS) and can't perform your job duties because of a disability that is likely to be permanent, you may be eligible for VRS disability retirement benefits. When applying, your application must include a Physician's Report (VRS-6B) form and copies of medical evidence related to your disabling condition(s); however, submission of a Physician's Report and copies of your doctors' medical records may not be enough to prove your claim. Read on to learn why.

The Physician's Report (VRS-6B) is not well designed to gather the information necessary to prove your claim

VRS will tell you its Physician's Report (VRS-6B) form allows your physician to provide VRS with information about your condition, and that submission of this form with copies of your doctors' medical records will give the VRS Medical Board the information it needs to understand how your illness impacts your job performance. However, this often isn't the case!

The opinions of a treating physician can be crucial in proving you are eligible to receive VRS disability retirement benefits; unfortunately, the Physician's Report (VRS-6B) form is not well designed to gather the information necessary to prove your claim.

Poor description of your functional limitations:

PART A. DESCRIPTION OF DISABLING ILLNESS

3. List the physical functional limitations preventing the applicant from performing his or her usual work duties:

Here is how Question 3 falls short and usually does not draw out the information necessary to prove your claim:

- Your doctor may not recall/recognize all your functional limitations unless the doctor is asked about a specific functional activity. (For example, "How long can your patient sit and stand/walk at one time and total in an 8-hour working day? Will your patient sometimes need to take unscheduled breaks during a working day?") The answers to these questions (and many others) about your functional limitations often go unreported on the Physician's Report (VRS-6B) form.

- Your doctor may never have reviewed your job description and may not be aware of all your usual work duties, and therefore may not recognize how the symptoms that result from your diagnosed conditions cause or contribute to your disability. It's a good idea to provide your doctor with a copy of your job description, as it may be impossible to prove your claim without it!

- The Physician's Report asks your doctor to list the functional limitations preventing you from performing your usual work duties, but doesn't describe your usual work duties for your doctor. Again, provide your doctor with a copy of your job description!

- Doctors often don't respond to Question 3 with complete sentences, much less a well thought out response which points to objective medical evidence in your record that supports the doctor's opinions. Results of an examination, lab tests, operative reports, echocardiograms, ultrasounds, pulmonary function tests, treadmill tests, x-rays, CTs, or MRIs are examples of objective medical evidence. The more your doctor points to objective medical evidence in support of his or her opinions, the greater the strength of the medical opinion and the stronger your claim.

- Question 3 does not ask about any cognitive impairments preventing you from performing your usual work duties. Your inability to do your job may be the result of a physical illness or injury, and/or a cognitive condition. (A cognitive disability is a loss or deterioration in intellectual capacity, and may occur as result of a stroke or Alzheimer's disease.) However, Question 3 does not ask about any cognitive impairments. Your doctor must find another way to describe any cognitive impairments which may be preventing you from performing your usual work duties.

- Finally, a thorough and complete response to Question 3 requires more space than the 11.12 square inch area provided on the form. The small area in which to respond often discourages your physician from providing a thorough and complete response to the question!

Your doctor's unfamiliarity with how your conditions cause or contribute to your disability:

Let's take a look at Question 4:

PART B. DIAGNOSIS AND TREATMENT

4. Indicate the diagnosis(es) and the onset date (for each), and whether each is causing or contributing to the disability:

Diagnosis (Full diagnostic description)	Date of Onset	Causing or Contributing?
_____	_____	_____
_____	_____	_____
_____	_____	_____
_____	_____	_____

- Again, if your doctor has never reviewed your job description he or she will likely not be aware of all your usual work duties, and therefore may not recognize how the symptoms that result from your diagnosed conditions cause or contribute to your disability. Again, this is why it is critical to provide your doctor with a copy of your job description!

Seemingly straightforward questions present possible pitfalls:

5. Date the patient became unable to work:

- Your doctor may not have been treating you at the time you became unable to work, and may only list the first day the doctor saw you. If the doctor responds with a date earlier than your first visit to the doctor, this response may reduce the doctor's credibility with those deciding your claim. If the doctor responds with a date after your date of retirement, this response will not be helpful, and could potentially torpedo your claim! Ideally, your doctor will respond by explaining the basis of his or her answer (i.e., review of your medical records, an acute medical event) and not just respond with a date.

An incomplete request for a description of your objective findings:

---

8. List the initial objective findings:

- While Question 8 seems pretty straightforward, you may have developed additional objective findings after your initial visit with your doctor, which would not be listed in response to this question or anywhere on the Physician's Report. As mentioned previously, the more your doctor points to objective medical evidence in support of his or her opinions, the greater the strength of the medical opinion and the stronger your claim. You'll see this theme repeatedly, because it can make or break your case!

A critical omission from Question 10:

10. List all current medications:			
Medication	Dosage	Duration	Patient Compliance?
_____	_____	_____	_____
_____	_____	_____	_____
_____	_____	_____	_____
_____	_____	_____	_____
_____	_____	_____	_____

- Question 10 does not ask about any side effects of your medications which may prevent you from performing your usual work duties. In fact, the Physician's Report form does not ask about side effects of medications at all! It is entirely up to your doctor to make sure these side effects are considered in your case.

Vague questions can lead to vague answers:

---

12. What improvement can be expected within one year of treatment?

- Question 12 is vague and does not specifically ask about the expected improvement in your ability to perform your usual work duties-- but that is the ultimate question: whether you'll improve enough to be able to resume working! Question 12 may distract your doctor from the real point of the form, and could easily sink your claim!

What's the problem with Questions 13 and 14?

13. Report any hospitalizations including special tests and or examinations for heart, vision and radiology:
14. Describe any surgical procedures performed on the patient including name, description of procedure, and response:

- Your doctor may provide an incomplete answer, which damages his or her credibility.

- Your doctor may not be aware of all your surgical procedures or your response to those procedures, and may provide an incomplete answer, which damages his or her credibility.

- Your doctor is busy and likely will not want to take the time to review your medical record thoroughly enough to provide a detailed and accurate response to these questions.

Question 16—One Of The Most Important Questions On The Form:

| 16. | Do you consider the patient's disabling condition(s) likely to be permanent? |
| | ❑ Yes   ❑ No |

- Your doctor may never have reviewed your job description and may not be aware of all your usual work duties, and therefore may not recognize how the symptoms that result from your diagnosed conditions cause or contribute to your disability. Get your doctor a copy of your job description—ASAP!

- Your doctor may be reluctant to take a position on whether or not your disabling condition(s) are likely to be permanent. Your doctor's main objective is to help improve your health and restore your functional abilities. Your doctor may feel that an affirmative response to this question is an admission of defeat, or may become a self-fulfilling prophecy. Doctors often like to keep an optimistic outlook and to take a wait and see approach. Surgeons sometimes have a high opinion of their surgical skills and like to think (especially if they have performed surgery on you) that you should definitely get better. Unfortunately, despite their best efforts, doctors are sometimes unable to restore an individual's ability to perform his or her usual work duties. *If it is more likely than not that you will not be able to perform your usual work duties in the future, your doctor should respond "Yes" to this question.* A "No", "Unsure", or "Unknown" response to this question can have a very negative impact on your claim!

- Doctors are often concerned that if they take a position, they will be challenged or cross-examined and they just don't want to be dragged into a controversy. However, unless you can afford to pay your doctor to appear at an informal fact-finding hearing, it is extremely unlikely that he or she will ever be questioned about the written opinions they provide.

- **Question 16 should really read, "Do you think, more likely than not, your patient will be permanently prevented from performing his or her usual work duties in a competitive work setting?"** This modified question focuses more appropriately on the main issue in your claim for VRS disability retirement benefits, and also relays that the standard of proof is a preponderance of the evidence or "more likely than not." Being "disabled" for VRS purposes does not mean total incapacity; however, you must be permanently prevented from performing your usual work duties. Also, **some doctors may erroneously think that their opinions must be "beyond a reasonable doubt" or to a "medical certainty." This is not correct; "more likely than not" is all that is required for a valid opinion.**

Medical Records Are Created For Treatment Purposes—Not For Documenting Your Claim For Disability

PART D. DOCUMENTATION REQUIRED TO SUBSTANTIATE CLAIMS

If the disability application is based on any of the conditions listed in this section, the following documentation is *required* where pertinent to the disability. Place a check by the type of condition and by all attachments being submitted.

If the disability application is *not* based on any of the conditions listed in this section, the physician's responsibility remains to provide any documentation such as consultations, radiology reports, other reports, special tests, laboratory or diagnostic studies and support the diagnosis.

- Yes, there's a problem with Part D too! PART D is below where your doctor signs the Physician's Report and is sometimes overlooked by the doctor and left incomplete.

- Also, **providing copies of your medical records alone will generally not provide enough information about how your symptoms limit your ability to perform your usual work duties on a full-time basis.** After all, the records are created for treatment purposes and not for documenting your claim for disability.

As you can see, proving eligibility for VRS disability retirement benefits is not as easy as it may seem at first. Submitting a Physician's Report (VRS-6B) form and copies of medical evidence just may not be enough for you to prove your claim. If you intend to apply for Virginia Retirement System disability retirement benefits, or have already done so, I believe having an attorney experienced in VRS disability claims on your side is a good idea. Frankly, I believe it is one area of the law where consumers actually need an attorney on their side from the very beginning.

My representation of you can begin even before you file your application for benefits. Many people contact me because they are thinking of filing a claim for disability. These people benefit greatly by contacting me at this early stage because they have not yet made any fatal mistakes! I've even encouraged some individuals to return to work when I could see that they didn't have a viable claim—and as a result, they saved their jobs, health insurance, and other benefits!

My work becomes more difficult (and expensive) if you have already made mistakes in filling out the VRS forms, or if your doctor has filled out the

Physician's Report (VRS-6B) form without knowing the information discussed in this report. Recently, for example, I reviewed a file where the physician responded to Question 16 with "Not certain." As discussed above, the doctor didn't understand that "more likely than not" is all that is required for a valid opinion. Unfortunately, the doctor put the brakes on this claim before it has even crossed the starting line! If the doctor had understood the information in this report, the slow start to this claim could have been prevented!

If your disability retirement application has already been denied, I can help you by reviewing the facts of your case, guiding you through the appeals process, developing a strategy or theory of your case, and gathering the evidence necessary to prove your claim. I can also provide you with questionnaires to help you obtain the critical information and opinions you need from your doctors to prove your claim.

If you plan to retain an attorney to assist you with your claim, it is best to get the attorney involved as early as possible. You want to give your attorney the greatest time and opportunity to help you! You also want the opportunity to put your strongest case forward as early on in the process as possible, in an effort to prove your claim and avoid the necessity and delay of an appeal. **Finally, if you wait until after you have had your informal fact-finding proceeding and been denied, it is highly unlikely that an attorney will be able to help you salvage your claim.**

About the Author

Brian J. Gillette is a disability attorney in Williamsburg, Virginia. In practice since 1992, he and his firm help people make smart decisions to improve their lives. He focuses his practice on representing individuals seeking Social Security and Virginia Retirement System (VRS) disability benefits throughout the Commonwealth of Virginia. Brian is also a Member of the Board of Governors of the Virginia Trial Lawyers Association and the Chair of the Virginia Trial Lawyers Association, Social Security Law Section. His firm, Gillette Law Group, PLLC, has twice been recognized by Coastal Virginia Magazine as a winner of its "Best of Coastal Virginia Readers' Choice Awards."

Brian was born in Washington, D.C., grew up in the Maryland suburbs, and attended law school at The College of William and Mary in Virginia. His mother was an elementary school teacher and principal, and his father recently retired from a firm that helps individuals with prosthetic devices. Brian is married with four children. He currently volunteers his time as Chairman of the Board of Directors of the Center for Child and Family Services, Inc., based in Hampton, Virginia, and also serves on the Board of the Bon Secours Mary Immaculate Foundation which raises funds to allow Bon Secours Mary Immaculate Hospital in Newport News, Virginia to offer services to the community that might not otherwise be possible.

PHYSICIAN'S REPORT

VIRGINIA RETIREMENT SYSTEM
P.O. Box 2500 • Richmond, VA 23218-2500
Toll-free 1-888-827-3847
Fax 804-786-9718
www.varetire.org

1. Social Security Number
2. Name

physician or other medical professional completes this form to describe the patient's illness(es) or condition(s) that qualify the applicant for disability retirement. This information is used to make a decision about the applicant's ability retirement application.

e: Review Part D to ensure all information supporting the diagnosis and treatment are submitted with this report.

RT A. DESCRIPTION OF DISABLING ILLNESS

List the physical functional limitations preventing the applicant from performing his or her usual work duties:

RT B. DIAGNOSIS AND TREATMENT

Indicate the diagnosis(es) and the onset date (for each), and whether each is causing or contributing to the disability:

Diagnosis (Full diagnostic description)	Date of Onset	Causing or Contributing?

Date the patient became unable to work:

Date of patient's most recent visit (which must have been within the last 6 months):

Date of patient's first visit pertaining to this disability:

List the initial objective findings:

6B (Rev. 01/19)

9. SSN

10. List all current medications:

Medication	Dosage	Duration	Patient Compliance

11. Description of any other treatment including therapy, patient compliance and response:

12. What improvement can be expected within one year of treatment?

13. Report any hospitalizations including special tests and or examinations for heart, vision and radiology:

14. Describe any surgical procedures performed on the patient including name, description of procedure, and response:

15. How has the patient's condition improved, remained unchanged, or worsened over the past year?

16. Do you consider the patient's disabling condition(s) likely to be permanent?
     ❑ Yes   ❑ No

VRS-6B (Rev. 01/19)

17. SSN

PART C. MEDICAL PROFESSIONAL INFORMATION

18. Name of Practice

19. Medical Professional's Name   (First, Middle Initial, Last)

20. Mailing Address   (Street, City, State and ZIP+4)

21. Telephone Number

22. Medical Professional Signature

NOTE: Unless otherwise specified, the Virginia Retirement System will *not* assume any responsibility for payment of fees for furnishing the requested information.

_____   _____
Signature   Date

PART D. DOCUMENTATION REQUIRED TO SUBSTANTIATE CLAIMS

If the disability application is based on any of the conditions listed in this section, the following documentation is *required* where pertinent to the disability. Place a check by the type of condition and by all attachments being submitted.

If the disability application is *not* based on any of the conditions listed in this section, the physician's responsibility remains to provide any documentation such as consultations, radiology reports, other reports, special tests, laboratory or diagnostic studies and support the diagnosis.

Musculo-Skeletal

- ❑ Report on any surgical treatment, including name of procedure and/or copy of operative note
- ❑ Current comprehensive Orthopedic examination
- ❑ Report on rheumatoid factor and sedimentation rate
- ❑ Report on uric acid relative to gouty arthritis
- ❑ Physical finding for all joints involved, including any deformities, tissue and bone destruction, range of motion and limitation of motion
- ❑ Current reports of radiology reports of involved joints

Cardiac

- ❑ EKG and echocardiograms
- ❑ Reports on exercise tolerance and stress
- ❑ Answers to the following questions: Is the patient able to climb one flight of steps or walk 200 yards on level ground? Do such activities bring on severe dyspnea and/or angina? Or what duration of physical activity can the patient tolerate?
- ❑ Location of edema
- ❑ Report of any other physical findings

Cancer

- ❑ Report on the stage of cancer
- ❑ Treatment Plan
- ❑ Oncology report
- ❑ CT scans
- ❑ Bone scans
- ❑ Lab Results

VRS-6B (Rev. 01/19)

23. SSN

❏ **Respiratory**

- ❏ Frequency, duration and severity of acute attacks of asthma, bronchitis, etc.
- ❏ Answer to the following question: Is the patient able to climb a flight of stairs or walk 100 yards without dyspnea
- ❏ Frequency of emergency room visits or hospitalization each year
- ❏ Report of current pulmonary function studies, predicted and actual values with the results expressed in the CC or liters and also in percent. Include the oxygen and carbon dioxide level of room air.

❏ **Neurological**

- ❏ Current comprehensive neurological examination dated within the last six months
- ❏ If the condition is a seizure disorder, give the frequency and severity of the seizures in the past year
- ❏ Report on current EEGs, CT scans, MRIs with dates
- ❏ Report on any of the following conditions which are present, indicating severity, distribution, and residual function in affected parts: Atrophy, paralysis, hemiplegia, impaired speech, tremors, gait, reflexes, and mental disturbances (including a report on cognitive ability)

❏ **Psychiatric**

- ❏ Psychiatric signs and symptoms
- ❏ Report of current psychiatric consultation to include disabling symptoms, diagnosis, treatment, and prognosis
- ❏ Number of appointments with psychiatrist, psychologist or medical social worker in the past two-year period and date of last appointment

❏ **Diabetes**

- ❏ Symptoms and complications
- ❏ History including onset date, length of treatment, and weight loss
- ❏ Current treatment, including insulin and medications
- ❏ Report on current blood sugars with date and/or A1C
- ❏ Report on current urinalysis with date

❏ **Visual**

- ❏ Report on visual acuity after best correction: R 20/_____ and L 20/_____
- ❏ Report of visual fields, including chart, if indicated
- ❏ Report on fundascopic findings
- ❏ Description of ocular tension
- ❏ Description of therapy and prognosis
- ❏ Information about whether or not the patient drives an automobile

❏ **Auditory-Vestibular**

- ❏ MRI or CT reports
- ❏ Audiogram with respect to puretone, SRT, and speech discrimination
- ❏ If patient has hearing aids, indicate the aided thresholds with respect to SRT and speech discrimination
- ❏ If vertigo or Menieres disease:
  - o Frequency, duration and severity of attacks
  - o ENG report
  - o Report on vestibular function and gait
  - o Report of any medical and surgical treatment

❏ **Digestive**

- ❏ Report on symptoms and treatment
- ❏ Endoscopies, radiological reports, and special studies
- ❏ Complete report of current lower or upper GI series with date, if pertinent

❏ **Fibromyalgia**

- ❏ Report of any tender points
- ❏ A functional capacity evaluation for the patient's job
- ❏ Psychiatric report, if applicable

❏ **Other** (Describe all documentation enclosed such as test results, consultation notes.)

VRS-6B (Rev. 01/19)